P9-BYR-091

DATE DUE			

940.4
MUR

31286111052699
Murphy, Jim.

**Truce : the day the
soldiers stopped
fighting**

**SIMSBURY HIGH SCHOOL LMC
SIMSBURY, CT 06070**

756100 01699   40159D   0001

TRUCE

THE DAY THE SOLDIERS STOPPED FIGHTING

JIM MURPHY

940.4
MUR

SIMSBURY HS SIMSBURY CT 06070

3128611052699   940.4 MUR
Truce : the day the soldiers

SCHOLASTIC PRESS • NEW YORK

Simsbury High School Library Media Center
34 Farms Village Road
Simsbury, CT 06070

Copyright © 2009 by Jim Murphy

All rights reserved. Published by Scholastic Press, an imprint of Scholastic Inc. *Publishers since 1920.* SCHOLASTIC, SCHOLASTIC PRESS, and associated logos are trademarks and/or registered trademarks of Scholastic Inc. No part of this publication may be reproduced, stored in a retrieval system, or transmitted in any form or by any means, electronic, mechanical, photocopying, recording, or otherwise, without written permission of the publisher. For information regarding permission, write to Scholastic Inc., Attention: Permissions Department, 557 Broadway, New York, NY 10012.

LIBRARY OF CONGRESS CATALOGING-IN-PUBLICATION DATA

Murphy, Jim, 1947–

Truce: the day the soldiers stopped fighting / by Jim Murphy.   p.   cm.

Includes bibliographical references.

ISBN-13: 978-0-545-13049-3 (hardcover)

ISBN-10: 0-545-13049-2 (hardcover)

1. Christmas Truce, 1914 — Juvenile literature.   2. World War, 1914–1918 — Campaigns — Western Front — Juvenile literature.   3. World War, 1914–1918 — Armistices — Juvenile literature.   I. Title.   D530.M87 2009

940.4'21 — dc22   2008040500

10   9   8   7   6   5   4   3   09   10   11   12   13

Printed in Singapore   46

First printing, October 2009

Text type was set in 16-pt Berkely Oldstyle Book.

Display type was set in OfficinaSan ITC Small Caps and Mrs. Eaves Small Caps.

Maps on pages 3, 16, 38, and 94 by Jim McMahon

Cover art and design by Scott McKowen

Art direction and book design by Marijka Kostiw

TO NANCY GALLT AND CRAIG VIRDEN —

FOR

THEIR CONSTANT SUPPORT AND

CALMING INFLUENCE,

ALWAYS THOUGHTFUL AND WISE

COMMENTS AND SUGGESTIONS,

AND

THEIR FREQUENT INVITATIONS

TO BUSINESS LUNCHES.

CONTENTS

"WHAT WOULD HAPPEN, I WONDER, IF THE ARMIES SUDDENLY AND SIMULTANEOUSLY WENT ON STRIKE AND SAID SOME OTHER METHOD MUST BE FOUND OF SETTLING THE DISPUTE?"

—*Winston Churchill*

to his wife, Clementine,
November 23, 1914

Detail of British and German soldiers exchanging gifts during the Christmas Truce of 1914

(*ILLUSTRATED LONDON NEWS*/MARY EVANS PICTURE LIBRARY)

British horse-drawn artillery being rushed to the front line of battle (IMPERIAL WAR MUSEUM, Q6728)

PREFACE

On July 29, 1914, the world's peace was shattered as the artillery of Austria-Hungary began shelling the troops of the country to its south, Serbia. What followed was like a row of dominoes falling over, as one European country after another rushed into war. Austria-Hungary's very powerful ally, Germany, joined it four days later to declare war on its neighbors and hurried troops across its borders into Belgium, Luxembourg, and Poland.

Against Austria and Germany stood France, Great Britain, Russia, and their many colonies and allies. The war widened in the months and years ahead until almost all of Europe was fighting. Even such faraway nations as Australia, Japan, and the United States were eventually drawn into the conflict. The soldiers who fought in this calamitous war called it the Great War. We know it today as the First World War.

None of the soldiers who joined this war knew how deadly or senseless it would be. They went off with great enthusiasm, determined to defend their countries' honor and to defeat an evil enemy. A young German student, Walter Limmer, wrote home just before he boarded a train heading for the front line of battle: "My dear ones, be proud that you live in such times and in such a nation, and that you have the privilege of sending several of those you love into this glorious struggle."

Their opponents were equally eager to get into the fight. "It is awful," declared Dougan Chater in England, "but one thing, it's got to happen some time, & best to have it while we are strong & have a good chance of whacking them."

In a matter of days, six million soldiers would find themselves facing weapons of unimaginable destructive power. Many of them would be blasted from the face of the earth, while others would be left permanently wounded in horrible ways. None of these young men realized that their leaders had lied to get them to fight in a war that did not have to happen. Nor could they know that on December 25, 1914, they would openly defy their commanding officers and meet on the battlefield in what can only be described as a Christmas miracle.

TRUCE

THE DAY THE SOLDIERS STOPPED FIGHTING

THOSE STUPID KINGS AND EMPERORS

As the twentieth century began, much of Europe was restless and fearful. For over forty years, countries had eyed one another suspiciously and prepared for a fight. By 1914, Europe was an armed camp ready to explode.

No single event caused the First World War. Rather, a series of big and small events slowly pushed all of the nations involved toward war. And even though we now know that the conflict might have been avoided, at the time, each country believed it had good reasons to fight.

For instance, in 1914, Germany was probably the most powerful country in Europe economically and militarily. But Germany's ruler, Kaiser Wilhelm II, was nervous. He believed that countries such as France and England had ignored his advice when it came to European politics. In addition, England, France, and Russia had formed an alliance, called the Triple Entente, early in the twentieth century. As a result, Wilhelm worried about his empire being

Kaiser Wilhelm II poses in his military uniform.

(THE GRANGER COLLECTION)

surrounded by unfriendly countries. For Wilhelm, his fears led him to rely on German military power to avoid being bullied.

Meanwhile, Wilhelm's Austrian ally, Emperor Franz Josef, was upset by the way Serbia was gaining economic and military power along his southern border. Two recent wars had more than doubled the size of that country. Franz Josef also knew that landlocked Serbia was looking for a shipping port on the Adriatic Sea. To accomplish this, Serbia was openly encouraging Serbs living in Bosnia-Herzegovina to break free from Austrian rule. Finally, Franz Josef was also eager to expand his empire to the east by taking control of parts of Poland. This perceived encroachment of Serbia and Austrian ambition made the emperor and his military advisors nervous and ready for war.

On the other side, France was tensed and anxious. The country was still nursing a grudge over being invaded and defeated in battle by Germany during the Franco-Prussian War of 1870–1871. The humiliation was made worse when France was forced to give Germany two of its territories on its eastern border, Alsace and Lorraine. Over in Great Britain, King George V and his parliament worried about Germany's growing naval power. This threatened England's dominance of the world's oceans and, in turn, its hold on its foreign colonies. Meanwhile in Russia, Czar Nicholas II had learned that both Germany and

Europe before the start of the war

Austria had moved troops near his border, and he grew anxious about a possible invasion of Poland, which was part of the Russian Empire. In addition, he hoped a strong Serbia would limit the growth of the Austro-Hungarian Empire in the south.

These jealousies, tensions, and ambitions had festered for many years — in the case of France, for more than forty years. With this kind of continual squabbling and suspicion, there was a real sense among the leaders and military commanders of these countries that a major conflict was very likely, if not inevitable.

Of course, in order to wage a successful war, they all knew they needed something else: the full support of their citizens. As one official German document bluntly put it, "We must accustom [our people] to think that an offensive war on our part is a necessity in order to combat the provocations of our adversaries."

To make sure this happened, the German government planted hundreds of articles in newspapers all across Germany alerting its people to the dangers posed by France, Great Britain, and Russia. At the same time, other articles and books celebrated their German culture and suggested that Germans were superior to any other people in the world. One writer, Theodore Springman, boldly proclaimed that once their enemies had been conquered, "Germany should civilize and Germanize the world."

These writings also painted an unflattering picture of other Europeans, suggesting that Russians were uncouth barbarians and that the French and British were decadent and un-Christian. The

Every country produced propaganda against its enemies. This French cartoon, called "Down with the Monster," shows a small group of brave soldiers confronting a giant, vicious dragon that represents Germany. (THE GRANGER COLLECTION)

attacks on Great Britain were particularly vicious. One of the most popular poems of the era was by Ernst Lissauer entitled *Hassgesang gegen England* — "Hymn of Hatred Against England."

The British and French did much the same thing to Germany and Austria, frequently referring to them as militaristic bullies. "The Prussian Junker," proclaimed Prime Minister Lloyd George before the English parliament, "is the road-hog of Europe. Small nationalities in his way are flung to the roadside, bleeding and broken." Pictures in French papers portrayed German soldiers as monsters rushing to destroy innocent civilians. It was also common to refer to them as Huns (a reference to Attila the Hun and the atrocities committed by his followers) and the Boche (a slang term for Germans that comes from the Old French word *caboche*, or hardhead).

Years of such government propaganda on each side conditioned European people to distrust and hate their enemies, many of whom longed for war. The campaigns were so successful that even India's staunch pacifist, Mahatma Gandhi, believed "it was our duty . . . to stand by [the English people] in their hour of need."

The situation came to a boil on the morning of June 28, 1914. While visiting Bosnia-Herzegovina, the heir to the Austrian Empire, Archduke Franz Ferdinand, and his wife were assassinated.

A dramatic painting showing the assassination of Archduke Franz Ferdinand and his wife in Sarajevo, Boznia-Herzegovina (THE GRANGER COLLECTION)

FELIX
SCHWORMSTADT
30 Juni 14

While the killings shocked most people, few expected they would lead to war. The murders had occurred inside the Austrian Empire, and no other country had claimed credit for the act. What is more, the Emperor of Austria, Franz Josef, was not at all unhappy that his nephew would no longer succeed him.

Franz Ferdinand had disappointed his uncle when he broke from tradition and married a commoner. Then he angered his uncle even more by announcing that he planned to give the Slavic minorities in the empire greater freedom once he became emperor himself. But now, with Franz Ferdinand dead, Franz Josef quickly recognized his less troublesome great-nephew, the Archduke Charles, as his new successor. The emperor was so pleased that he remarked, "For me it is a great relief from worry."

But Franz Josef's military advisors believed the assassinations were part of a Serbian conspiracy to incite rebellion in Bosnia-Herzegovina. Fueled by anti-Serbian riots throughout the empire, his advisors demanded action. They were encouraged in this by Kaiser Wilhelm. In a June 30 telegram, the kaiser made his hopes very clear: "The Serbs must be disposed of, and that right soon!"

Franz Josef hesitated. He was afraid that an attack on Serbia would force Russia to respond militarily. Germany reassured him that Russia was "in no way prepared for war," but that "should war between Austria-Hungary and Russia prove unavoidable," Germany would be at Austria's side immediately.

Several days went by, but Franz Josef still did not act. In part, this was due to his cautious nature. But it was also the result of a secret report he'd received the day before. This report clearly stated that there was no evidence that the Serbian government had been involved in the assassinations.

Franz Josef did not make the report public, so the pressure from his advisors and citizens to attack continued. Kaiser Wilhelm even egged him on with a private message that read, "The earlier Austria attacks the better. It would have been better to attack yesterday than today; and better to attack today than tomorrow."

Prodded by public opinion, his advisors, Kaiser Wilhelm, and his fear of Serbian expansion, Franz Josef decided to ignore the secret report and force a confrontation. On July 23, Austria issued an ultimatum to Serbia containing fifteen demands. Among the demands, Serbia was required to stop all anti-Austrian propaganda, abandon its activities in Bosnia-Herzegovina, and allow Austria to join in the investigation, trial, and punishment of the murders. An answer was demanded within forty-eight hours.

Acceptance of the demands would require Serbia to give up a great deal of its national authority, so no one expected it to agree to the harsh terms. Countries began calling up their soldiers and moving them into position. Everyone expected war.

Then something truly surprising happened.

Serbia replied to the ultimatum on July 25. The nation agreed to all of the provisions except one, Austria's insistence that it participate in the Serbian judicial process. But even in this matter, the Serbian government was agreeable. They suggested instead that the issue be submitted to a court at The Hague in neutral Holland that had been established to settle international disputes.

This news brought a sense of relief to many countries. War, it seemed, had been averted. Unfortunately, Franz Josef would have none of it. Because of Germany's strong encouragement and reassurances, the emperor was now fully committed to invading Serbia.

On July 28, the Austrian army marched to Serbia's border and set up its artillery. As this was taking place, Kaiser Wilhelm picked up the full text of Serbia's reply to Austria's ultimatum. Incredibly, he hadn't bothered to study it before, preferring to let his advisors read and interpret it for him. What he read astonished him so much that he hastily scribbled in the margin of the Serbian reply: "A great moral victory for Vienna; but with it every reason for war is removed. . . . On the strength of this I should never have ordered mobilization."

Wilhelm then shot off an urgent message to his foreign diplomat in Austria in an effort to avert war. But it was too late. Austrian artillery began shelling Serbian troops on July 29, setting other armies in Europe into rapid motion.

Only those at the highest levels of government knew that the war could have been avoided. One such person was forty-year-old Winston Churchill, who was in charge of the British navy at the time. When he learned that fighting had started, he dashed off an angry note to his wife: "I wondered whether those stupid Kings and Emperors could not assemble together and [revive] kingship by saving the nations from hell. . . ."

But Churchill was a realist, and he knew that the rush to war had been driven by the egos and ambitions of their national leaders, fueled by misguided popular support. Almost with a sigh, he concluded, "We all drift along in a kind of dull . . . trance. As if it was somebody else's operation."

German troops advancing through northeastern France during August 1914 (IMPERIAL WAR MUSEUM, Q53422)

THINGS WERE BEGINNING TO LOOK UNPLEASANT

Once set in motion, each country's army moved with surprising speed. Cavalry units galloped up country roads, their sabers rattling at their sides. Following them came thundering lines of horse-drawn artillery. Endless parades of soldiers tramped across dusty fields, eager to take on the enemy.

After several days of constant shelling, the Austrian army crossed the River Sava and entered the Serbian capital of Belgrade. Russia divided up its huge force to form two separate armies. One took on the Germans in northern Poland, while the other went south to confront Austrian forces in Galicia. The British hastily landed 120,000 men and rushed them north to join with French and Belgian troops trying to stop the Germans before they entered France.

Meanwhile, the actions of two armies had been prearranged for many years. Germany wanted to avoid a series of heavily armed forts that protected the French border. To accomplish this, it followed a plan devised in 1905 by its former military commander, Alfred von Schlieffen. The Schlieffen Plan had most of Germany's

German troops being transported to the front from Alsace-Lorraine in August 1914

(THE GRANGER COLLECTION)

troops attacking France through neutral Belgium and then descending on Paris from the north. Once Paris had been taken, the army would turn around and attack Russia.

The French had their own blueprint for war, called Plan XVII. This directed that, at the outbreak of a conflict with Germany, at least half of the French army would immediately cross the German border in a number of places and retake Alsace-Lorraine. It would then press on to the German capital of Berlin.

By mid-August, fighting was taking place in many locations all over Europe. Meanwhile, enlistment centers in every country involved were crowded with eager volunteers clamoring to get into battle as quickly as possible. Not only did they want to

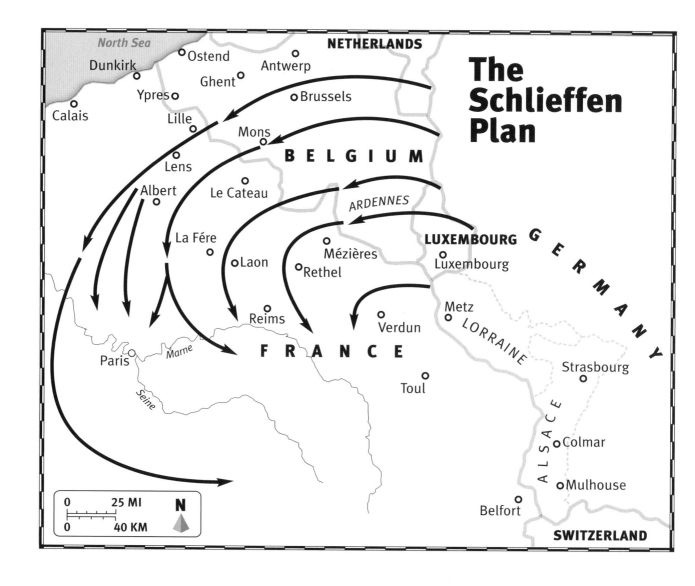

The Schlieffen Plan

defend their homelands, but these men were genuinely worried that the war would be over before they had a chance to fight.

The notion that this would be a brief war came from overly optimistic military leaders. According to Schlieffen, Paris could be occupied and France defeated within six weeks. Once France capitulated, other countries would sue for peace on Germany's terms. The French military allowed more time to complete Plan XVII, believing the German army could be defeated by Christmas. The soldiers marching off certainly shared this feeling.

A British citizen in Germany, Betty Cunliffe-Owen recalled, "The Germans left with the light of victory already in their eyes. . . . [Count Kanitz] promised to send a post card from Paris in a few weeks!" Harold Macmillan was a young, idealistic British lieutenant when the war began and expressed what most soldiers on both sides must have felt. "The general view," he wrote later, "was that it would be over by Christmas. Our major anxiety was by hook or crook not to miss it."

The idea that the war would be a quick and glorious adventure persisted through all the days leading up to the first major battle outside the industrial city of Mons, Belgium. Here, on August 23,

The Schlieffen Plan called for a number of German armies to sweep into France and capture Paris from the north.

An enthusiastic crowd of Englishmen lining up at the Whitechapel Recruiting Office

(IMPERIAL WAR MUSEUM, Q42033)

French, Belgian, and British forces (sometimes referred to as the Allies) came face-to-face with the advancing German army. A British artillery sergeant, Albert George, recalled looking across a wide valley at the enemy three miles away. "The order 'Action' came down," he remembered, "and everybody went to their different duties. . . ." Even though they were vastly outnumbered by the enemy, George remained naively confident and was still "very pleased to have a go at the Germans."

The battle began with an hour-long artillery duel, followed by a mass charge of German infantry across the open terrain. "Things were beginning to look unpleasant," George went on, "as we had to fire [our artillery] alternately at their infantry and [at their artillery], as our infantry had not arrived. At about 12:15 the German gunners found our battery and things were beginning to get very hot for us [as] shells were dropping all around us. . . ."

The British infantry finally arrived and waded into battle. "All that afternoon," George proudly reported, "we kept the Huns at bay although they [outnumbered us] ten to one."

But by midafternoon, it became clear that the sheer size of the German army meant it would eventually prevail. So after seven hours of vicious fighting, the Allied troops began pulling out of Mons.

Despite retreating, George and the troops around him were still enthusiastic. "Instead of being downcast, [our troops] were much impressed with the superiority of their rifle fire and . . . maneuvering over the enemy's fire and movements 'en masse.'" In their minds, they hadn't been beaten; they'd been driven back only because the enemy had more soldiers on the field. All they had to do was hold on until the men enlisting back home finally reached the battlefields.

After retreating for three days, French and British troops were ordered to make a stand at a small French village called Le Cateau. George was still "eager for the fray" and was pleased that his gun was positioned near the center of a four-mile-long line of artillery with the enemy guns in plain sight one mile away.

This artillery duel proved to be much more devastating than the one at Mons. George recalled that the enemy was soon "hitting our guns and wagons and killing most of the gunners. . . . We could see ammunition wagons trying to replenish [our guns] getting about half-way [to them], then a couple of shells would burst blowing the drivers and horses to smithereens. It was a terrible sight. . . ."

Word soon arrived from the Allied High Command. Even though the battle was clearly going against them, they were ordered to stand and fight. So George and his fellow artillerists continued loading and firing. "Every gun of our army was firing as fast as possible," George was quick to point out, "and by reports we did awful damage [to them], but the German guns [outnumbered us] 10 to 1 so you can imagine which had the best chance."

They were on the verge of complete collapse when the High Command finally relented and called a retreat. But this withdrawal was very different from the one at Mons. That one had been hasty but fairly well organized. This one at Le Cateau was sheer panic.

Exhausted French infantrymen in retreat (IMPERIAL WAR MUSEUM, Q109707)

Because the opposing armies had been so close to each other, the long-range artillery of the Germans could still drop shells onto the retreating soldiers when they were two and three miles from the village. "The retirement," George recounted bitterly, "was a scandalous sight in the History of Britain. . . . In our hurry to get away guns, wagons, horses, [and] wounded men were left to the victorious Germans and even our *British Infantrymen* were throwing away their rifles, ammunition, equipment and running *like hell* for their lives. . . ."

When these soldiers had rushed to enlist, they brought with them nineteenth-century ideas of what warfare would be like. Most men believed that battles were fought under gentlemanly (if unwritten) rules. One such "rule" suggested that enemies face each other openly in combat. What is more, their commanding officers had conducted the opening two battles using nineteenth-century tactics, which included attempting to overwhelm an enemy with mass charges of infantry. Unfortunately, now they were using twentieth-century weapons with truly terrible destructive powers.

By the beginning of World War I, all European armies had infantry rifles that were accurate up to one thousand yards. These, plus machine guns that could shoot between 100 and 500 rounds a minute, made it virtually impossible for a massed charge to succeed. Field artillery could fire a shell up to five miles in distance and were capable of unleashing twenty rounds a minute. Heavy artillery could lob shells with reasonable accuracy up to twenty-five miles. It was now possible for soldiers to come under a killing barrage and never really see the enemy.

During the years to follow, other highly lethal weapons joined these to wreak havoc on soldiers and civilians alike. They included airplanes and zeppelins armed with machine guns and bombs, armored tanks, flamethrowers, portable mortars, and poison gas. More important, military equipment and tactics had not evolved to match these more sophisticated weapons. No one had faced these

A German machine-gun regiment awaiting another charge in 1914 (THE GRANGER COLLECTION)

savage weapons in actual battle, so effective countermeasures had never been thought out and tested. As hard as it is to believe, most soldiers going into combat in 1914 didn't even have steel helmets to protect them from flying pieces of metal. In addition, the top commanders on both sides stuck with the notion that their troops were superior to the enemy's and could overcome any obstacle by sheer determination.

Following the battle at Le Cateau, the Allied forces retreated for nearly two weeks, all the while being pursued and attacked by the enemy. Captain E. L. Spears recalled watching French soldiers stumbling past him. "Heads down, red trousers and blue coats indistinguishable for the dust, bumping into [trucks], into abandoned carts, into each other, they shuffled down the endless roads, their eyes filled with dust that dimmed the scalding landscape, so that they saw clearly only the foreground of discarded packs, prostrate men, and an occasional abandoned gun."

The soldiers weren't the only ones suffering in the late summer heat. "Dead and dying horses," Spears added, "lay in great numbers by the side of the roads. Worse still, horses dying but not yet dead, sometimes struggling a little, a strange appeal in their eyes, looked at the passing columns whose dust covered them, caking their thirsty lips and nostrils."

In places the retreat covered almost 120 miles with the Germans coming within 30 miles of Paris. It appeared to everyone that the Germans would complete the conquest of France in a few

German long-range artillery decimated this supply train in a matter of minutes.
(AUTHOR'S COLLECTION)

weeks. Then, on September 4, the Allies carried out a desperate counterattack called the Battle of the Marne that finally halted the German advance. How could they have succeeded against such odds?

By this time, German soldiers — what was left of them — had been marching and fighting continuously for more than thirty days. Their commanders and officers had pushed so hard to fulfill the Schlieffen Plan that the advance forces were hundreds of miles from supply lines and reserve soldiers. This meant that these fatigued soldiers couldn't be replaced by fresh recruits. Instead, in addition to fighting, they'd had to travel on foot, carrying supplies, heavy equipment, and weapons, despite being exhausted and injured.

Adding to German woes was the fierce resistance put up by Belgian and French civilians. While these freedom fighters were no match for the highly trained and well-equipped German soldiers, they did force them to deploy thousands of troops to guard food and weapons supplies. By the beginning of September, the Germans were as much decimated and exhausted by their victories as the British, French, and Belgians were in defeat.

The Allied counterattack proved to be so successful that it began pushing back the German army. The Germans might have lost even more ground except that, as October neared, all of the countries involved in the war found themselves short on ammunition and men. Quite simply, there hadn't been enough time to take the most recent enlistees, arm and train them, and get them to the front lines of the war.

In the autumn days ahead, there would be more charges and countercharges. Heightening the misery was a series of torrential rainstorms, some lasting several days. By October, the armies had come to a grinding halt on every front. "The energies of [all warring] armies flagged," wrote historian John W. Wheeler-Bennett, "worn out by defeats, fighting, and the vileness of the [now] swampy country."

Fierce fighting continued, but no army seemed capable of driving back the enemy. Instead, soldiers struggled from village to village, then farm to farm, until the lines of battle seemed to hardly move at all. The closeness of the enemy and rising casualty rates forced the commanders of both sides to make a momentous decision. Soldiers would begin digging trenches to hide from the killing fire.

This happened in Serbia and Romania between the Austrian and Serbian/Russian forces. It happened in Poland and Galicia between German/Austrian troops and Russian troops. One of the most dramatic battle lines formed on what came to be called the Western Front.

Here two parallel trenches — one held by the Germans, the other by the French, English, and Belgians — from fifty to one thousand yards apart stretched from the North Sea coast all the way to the Swiss border, a total of over 475 miles. In between was a ravaged

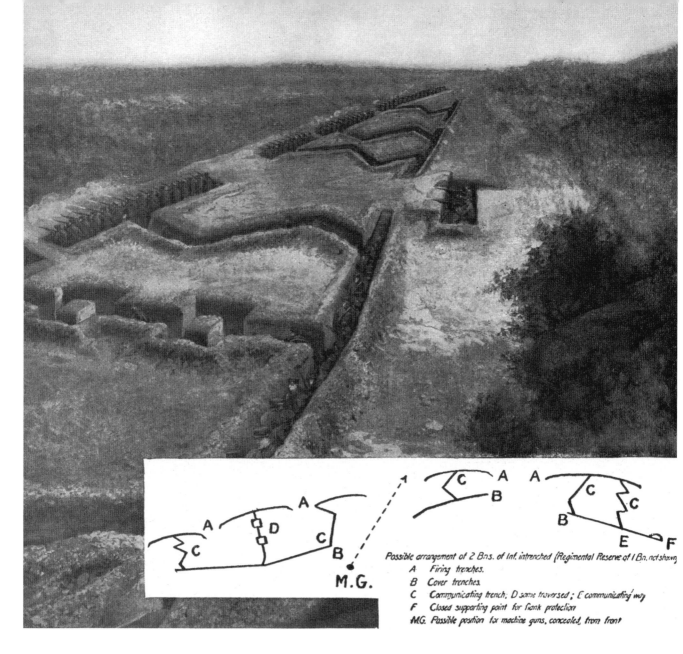

Possible arrangement of 2 Bns. of Inf. intrenched (Regimental Reserve of 1 Bn. not shown)
A   Firing trenches.
B   Cover trenches.
C   Communicating trench; D some traversed; E communicating way
F   Closed supporting point for flank protection
M.G. Possible position for machine guns, concealed, from front

Engineers designed trenches to be neat and tidy, such as these from an army training manual. In reality, most were hastily dug and poorly constructed holes in the ground. (AUTHOR'S COLLECTION)

wasteland crisscrossed by tangles of razor-sharp barbed wire and appropriately nicknamed No Man's Land. As the men on each side cautiously watched the enemy across from them, they understood that they had entered an altogether new kind of warfare.

THREE

ALL ATTACKS ARE TO BE PUSHED TO THE EXTREME

All along the Western Front, the soldiers on both sides now found themselves in a world that had been completely destroyed by machine-gun and artillery fire. A British major, Valentine Fleming, described the scene around him to his friend Winston Churchill: "Imagine a broad belt, ten miles or so in width . . . which is positively littered with the bodies of men . . . ; in which farms, villages and cottages are shapeless heaps of blackened masonry; in which fields, roads and trees are pitted and torn and twisted by shells and disfigured by dead horses, cattle, sheep and goats. . . ."

In this nightmare landscape the soldiers were forced to live in narrow, zigzagging dirt enclosures four feet wide and six or seven feet deep. The walls often collapsed, especially after bomb explosions shook the earth loose. During the summer, the sun could make the tight spaces as hot as an oven, while in winter a cold, damp wind would freeze fingers and toes. But in the fall of 1914, it was the series of fierce downpours that made everything a wet, muddy mess. Soldiers, Fleming went on to explain, crouched in the trenches "coated with mud, unshaven, hollow-eyed with continual

strain, unable to reply to the everlasting rain of shells hurled at them from three, four, five or more miles away. . . ."

The sound of artillery seemed to be ever present, with distant, echoing thuds being followed by massive explosions and flying debris. Often the firing went on day and night, disrupting sleep and keeping the men on edge constantly. Valentine Fleming felt the trenches were made "hideous by the incessant crash and whistle and roar of every sort of projectile."

Throughout November and into December, the weather stayed unusually warm and wet. "The rain pours incessantly from above," Friedrich Nickolaus told his family in Germany, "while beneath us

By early 1917, the landscape near Ypres has been pounded into desolation by long-range, heavy artillery. (IMPERIAL WAR MUSEUM, Q10711)

Constant rain and the movement of troops, artillery, and supply wagons
churned the earth into a muddy ooze. Here soldiers coax two mules forward
a step at a time near Ypres, Belgium. (IMPERIAL WAR MUSEUM, [AUS] 963)

the water-table has risen to just below ground level." Several
miles away, another German soldier, Karl Aldag, echoed
Nickolaus's feelings: "I must confess this life of slime and mud
often fills me with revulsion, also the never-ending wet, cold
and futile work."

Even when not experiencing a bombardment, the men in the trenches had to be extremely cautious. Both sides had sharp-shooters capable of picking off anyone who showed his head even for a split second. In addition, planes came swooping out of the clouds to machine-gun men as they scurried to find cover in the tight spaces.

There were other nonmilitary dangers to worry about as well. The dead humans and animals on the battlefield attracted swarms of hungry rats. Lice and fleas got into the men's clothing and bedding and made their lives miserable, while great clouds of black flies nipped at their faces and got into their nostrils and food.

And then there was illness and disease. Conditions in the trenches were so foul and unsanitary that hundreds of thousands of men sickened and died. Between 1914 and 1918, over 6,200,000 men would die in the trenches on the Western Front alone. More than half of them — 3,528,000 — died from one disease or another.

There was something else that plagued all of the soldiers involved — boredom. Even though both sides' forward lines were in clear view across the blasted terrain of No Man's Land, soldiers rarely saw the enemy. Because of the ever-present danger from snipers, everybody kept their heads down.

Days dragged along with little change in their routine. Soldiers

Miserable German soldiers in their gloomy trench early in the war

(THE GRANGER COLLECTION)

got up each morning, ate breakfast, stood in the trench, and waited, rifle at the ready, in case the enemy decided to charge. Because the trenches were so fragile, they needed constant attention and repair, which was always done at night when there was less chance of being spotted by a sniper.

Life in the trenches was miserable, but it did have an unforeseen positive consequence for the men that autumn. The muddy conditions, plus the shortage of men and ammunition, made it impossible for either side to organize and launch a major battle. For a very brief period in October, the number of soldiers killed each day actually went down.

Unfortunately, the commanders of the warring armies shared a hatred for this new situation. They worried that if their men sat around doing nothing they might lose their fighting edge. Besides, all the commanding officers believed that to win they had to destroy the morale of their opponents. The British infantry regulations stated very clearly that "a determined and steady advance lowers the fighting spirit of the enemy." Finally, there was a real feeling that to sit and defend a position was unmanly. One British commander, General William Robertson, observed that the defensive nature of trench warfare was "thought to be . . . obnoxious."

Those in charge of the armies were determined to "push forward" at any cost. Retired German cavalry officer Friedrich von Bernhardi emphasized the importance of staying on the offensive when he wrote, "There is *one* quality above all in man which is of the utmost importance in all warfare, and that really benefits the attack exclusively — boldness."

Wet, warm weather and the rotting corpses of men and animals created unsanitary conditions and disease. Here, dead German soldiers lie in their trench near the village of La Bassée, France. (AUTHOR'S COLLECTION)

This meant sending raiding parties into No Man's Land to attack the enemy's trench even in the face of modern weapons. "All attacks are to be pushed to the extreme," wrote French general Joseph Joffre, "with the firm resolution to charge the enemy with the bayonet, in order to destroy him."

But even if the enemy wasn't defeated or driven from his trenches, it didn't matter. As another French general, Ferdinand Foch, explained, simply making the charge was as important as winning because it kept the enemy nervous. "A battle won is one in which one will not confess oneself to be beaten. . . . To organize battle consists in enhancing our own spirit to the highest degree in order to break that of the enemy."

Over twenty-five miles behind the lines and safely away from the enemy's long-range artillery, the commanders on both sides frequently ordered their soldiers "over the top" in raids that were doomed before they started. As military historian John Ellis noted, "Machine guns and rifles must give almost the whole advantage to the defender. But the generals did not acknowledge this."

Raids came in two forms. The most common was carried out by an officer and one or two soldiers in the dead of night. A French soldier in the Argonne region of France recalled climbing out of the trench with two comrades. "We slid forward imperceptibly, moving on our elbows and knees, our left hands gripping the handle of our bayonets."

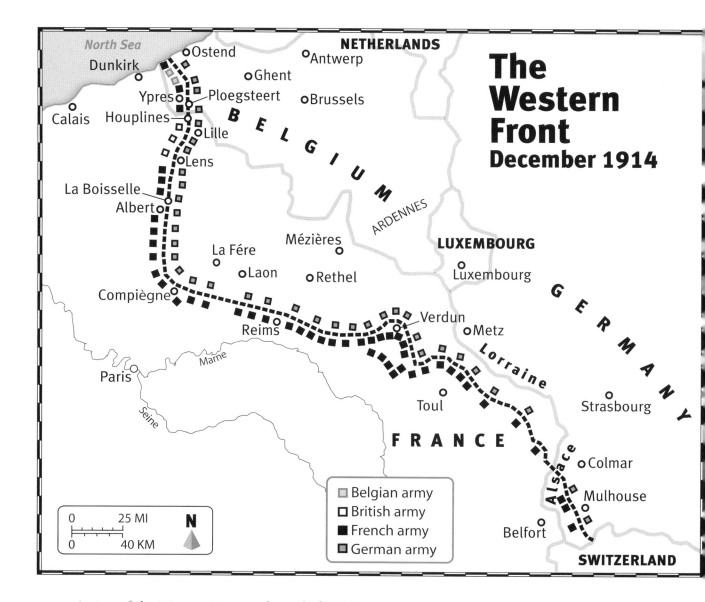

The Western Front
December 1914

North Sea

NETHERLANDS

Dunkirk
Ostend
Antwerp
Ghent
Calais
Ypres
Ploegsteert
Brussels
Houplines
Lille
BELGIUM
Lens
La Boisselle
Albert
ARDENNES
La Fére
Mézières
LUXEMBOURG
Laon
Rethel
Luxembourg
Compiègne
GERMANY
Reims
Verdun
Metz
Marne
Lorraine
Paris
Toul
Strasbourg
Seine
FRANCE
Alsace
Colmar
Mulhouse
Belfort
SWITZERLAND

0   25 MI
0   40 KM
N

Belgian army
British army
French army
German army

A view of the Western Front at the end of 1914

The man in the lead had to cut through the many strands of barbed wire they encountered. This was slow work since enemy guards were trained to shoot in the direction of any sound they heard. It might take an hour or longer to cover one hundred yards.

The main object of these small raids was to gather information about the enemy — to find out if their trenches were heavily defended or whether they were planning a raid of their own. Sometimes, if they got close enough without being detected, the men might lob grenades into the enemy trenches, then hightail it back across No Man's Land to safety.

The bigger raids were designed to drive the enemy from their trenches and could include thirty or more men. These raids required a great deal of planning and preparation and usually took place during the day.

On the day of the raid, the men lined up along the trench, ready to scramble over the parapet when ordered. Many mumbled prayers, while others struggled with intense private fears. Even though strict secrecy was ordered, everyone understood that the enemy probably knew a raid was coming.

How did they know? First, in order to provide a clear route across No Man's Land, the barbed wire had to be cut days in advance of the raid and the path marked with white ribbons. Then, on the morning of the attack, artillery would pound away at the section of enemy trench that was about to be stormed. As one British soldier remarked sarcastically, "The advertisement of the attack on our front was absurd. . . . Small wonder the machine-gun fire was directed with such fatal precision."

Every man involved knew that in a matter of minutes he would be

British soldiers await the order to "go over the top" and dash across No Man's Land.

(AUTHOR'S COLLECTION)

out in the open and an easy target for the enemy. Why would these men willingly put themselves in such an impossibly dangerous situation? As one British officer explained, "The honour of my battalion and its opinion of me . . . are now my sustaining motives in the game of war."

When the signal was finally given, "we climbed up our ladders and went forward," British private Alan Thomas recalled. "It was a strange sensation walking upright in No Man's Land when up till then you had only crawled. But I did not feel afraid or at least not nearly so afraid as I had felt immediately before going over."

The officers tried to keep the men together and moving in the right direction, a difficult thing to do under the circumstances. Private Thomas remembered "[t]he noise, the smoke, the smell of gunpowder, the rat-tat of rifle and machine-gun fire combined to numb the senses. I was aware of myself and others going forward, but of little else."

Onward they went, slipping in the mud, trying to avoid tripping over twisted pieces of jagged metal or falling into bomb craters. If a man wandered from the intended route, he could find himself tangled in sharp barbed wire and an easy target. "I moved past [the stumps of] trees," a British private would remember, "past other things; men passed by me, carrying other men, some crying, some cursing, some silent. They were all shadows, and I was no greater than they. Living and dead, all were alike. . . ."

"They were caught up in the sheer momentum of the forward rush," historian John Ellis explained, "an unthinking mass pushing forward until they were literally annihilated by the insuperable density of the opposing firepower."

While these raids often provided valuable military information, they rarely succeeded in driving the enemy from the trenches and almost always resulted in staggering casualties. It was not uncommon for half of the attacking force to either be killed or wounded. And yet, neither the extraordinary loss of life nor the fact that little was gained by these raids stopped commanders from

British soldiers charging across a heavily barbed-wired No Man's Land in 1916
(IMPERIAL WAR MUSEUM, Q70167)

ordering more of them. It's not surprising, then, that the men detested the raids. As one British soldier told it, "How these raids came to be abominated by those who had to make them! To judge from what appeared in some of the newspapers, as well as official communiqués . . . the British soldier longed above all things to be allowed to take part in a raid. If this was indeed the case he certainly concealed his desire very successfully from his friends."

The war dragged along into December with both sides making numerous raids and both sides taking heavy losses. Already, more than one million soldiers had been killed, with many more wounded. Worse still, there was no end to the war in sight. As Valentine Fleming remarked at the time, "It's going to be a *long war* in spite of the fact that on both sides every single man in it wants it stopped *at once*."

The men were exhausted physically and emotionally, and longed for some sort of resolution to the fighting. They sensed, too, that something dramatic had to take place. English lieutenant J. D. Wyatt felt this strongly: "Something must happen soon. The situation seems absurd — 2 huge armies sitting & watching each other like this."

Wyatt did not know it, but his wish would come true in just a few weeks.

The Tyneside Irish Brigade marching resolutely into withering enemy fire at La Boisselle, France. So many soldiers were killed or wounded during such charges that No Man's Land came to be called the Sausage Valley. (IMPERIAL WAR MUSEUM, Q53)

THERE IS NO LONGER ANY SENSE
IN THIS BUSINESS

The soldier's life on the Western Front was ruled by noise — the sound of artillery pounding away, the rat-tat of machine-gun fire, the drone of planes overhead, the shouting of orders. But there were times, especially at night, when a stretch of the trenches might take a break from fighting and absolute silence followed.

During these rare moments of quiet, most of the men tried to relax and possibly catch up on their sleep. Those still on duty soon discovered something amazing. They could hear the enemy in their trenches. Bits of conversations and bursts of laughter drifted across No Man's Land. The sound of a musical instrument and singing might be heard.

These incidental contacts with the enemy made each side curious. They had been induced to fight in part because they'd been led to believe the enemy was inferior to them or a mindless monster. What they were now hearing might be in a different language from theirs, but the sounds were still very familiar.

This impression was often confirmed by those going out on night patrols. In a letter to his wife in England, Lieutenant Colonel Laurence Fisher-Rowe reported that his friend "Jimmy went out

A group of Scottish soldiers and their mascot relax in the crowded front line trench.

(AUTHOR'S COLLECTION)

last night and says he could hear the Huns sloshing about in their trenches & coughing as much as we do, so I expect they are equally uncomfortable."

Another British soldier, Rifleman Leslie Walkinton, volunteered that sometimes he and his friends chatted with the enemy. "We used to shout remarks at each other, sometimes rude ones, but generally with less venom than a couple of London cab [drivers] after a mild collision."

Occasionally, the shouting matches even turned into friendly musical serenades. A young British private had fond memories of those in which he took part. "On a quiet night we used to sing to each other, sometimes alternate verses of the same tune. . . . They often sang their own words to the tune of 'God Save the King.'"

A German soldier puts out a target for a shooting match between British and German soldiers sometime in early December 1914. (*ILLUSTRATED LONDON NEWS*/MARY EVANS PICTURE LIBRARY)

In some areas of the front lines, more than just songs were shared. "We were so close," seventeen-year-old Albert Moren noted in a letter to his parents in London, "we threw tins of bully beef over to them or jam or biscuits and they threw things back. It wasn't done regularly, just an occasional sort of thing."

These friendly exchanges between enemies worried the commanding officers a great deal. English general Horace Smith-Dorrien wrote in his diary on December 2: "Weird stories in from the trenches about fraternizing with the Germans. They shout at each other and offer to exchange certain articles and give certain information. In one place, by arrangement, a bottle was put out between the trenches and then they held a competition to [see] which [side] could break it first!"

The notion of his troops getting along with the enemy so worried and annoyed Smith-Dorrien that he decided to put a stop to it: "I therefore intend to issue instructions to my Corps not to fraternize in any way whatever with the enemy for fear one day they may be lulled into such a state of confidence as to be caught off guard and rushed."

Lower-ranking officers responded to these new instructions. One British private recalled that often while singing to the enemy, "An officer of one side or the other would come up and stop [the singing] by ordering a few rounds of fire. We used to be sporting and fire high with the first round — and so did brother Boche."

The truth was that something deeper was at work on the men. The more friendly contact they had with the enemy, the less anger they felt toward them. After describing in detail how neighborly the enemy across from him was, German captain Rudolf Binding concluded his diary entry with, "Truly, there is no longer any sense in this business."

But most higher-ranking officers felt the business of war had to go on. Because fresh troops and ammunition began to arrive as winter came on, the British High Command decided to put a complete end to fraternization by launching a series of large-scale raids.

The first of these took place on December 14 at Somme in France and involved nearly two thousand men. Captain Billy Congreve watched from a nearby hill as the hastily thought-up and ill-prepared attack took place. "Imagine sending [soldiers] to attack a strongly wired position up a hill and over mud a foot deep, under frontal and [side] fire. It was a regular Valley of Death. . . . The attack naturally failed. We had about 400 casualties. It is most depressing."

Yet a week later, Congreve saw a newspaper report in which his commanders lied about the raid, boasting that it had been a complete success. His blood boiling, Congreve noted angrily, "A beautiful epitaph for those poor boys who were little better than murdered."

The German High Command retaliated with a sustained raid on British troops along the French and Belgian border near the North Sea. This battle lasted four days with thousands of casualties on both sides.

Another futile British charge
across No Man's Land

(AUTHOR'S COLLECTION)

More large-scale and fruitless attacks were made over the following two weeks, adding thousands of men to the lists of killed and wounded. These raids might have gone on indefinitely except that Christmas was approaching. The rulers and civilians back home wanted the men in the front lines to have some sort of Christmas cheer and sent thousands upon thousands of carefully prepared gift boxes to the battlefield. As the fighting stopped, British major G. D. Jeffreys grumped that "[E]verything seems hung up just now for all the Christmas parcels, which are becoming a positive nuisance. . . . Our enemy thinks of war, and nothing else, whilst we must mix it up with plum puddings!"

Jeffreys had no way of knowing it, of course, but the enemy was just as distracted by Christmas. His German counterpart, Captain Rudolf Binding, complained that "[I]f I had my way, some person in authority would proclaim that Christmas will not be celebrated this year. . . . Enemy, Death, and a Christmas tree — they cannot live so close together."

The soldiers, however, were ready for Christmas and a break from random death. The packages from home were opened eagerly, and puddings and sausages, pipes and tobacco, and other small gifts were shared with comrades. In addition to their holiday parcels, German soldiers received thousands of small pine trees decorated with candles.

As the spirit of the approaching holiday took hold, both sides began to sing Christmas carols during their nightly serenades.

Gradually, the tension and anger of the soldiers gave way to more peaceful thoughts. German Karl Aldag wrote to his parents, "We were relieved on the evening of the 23rd about 10 o'clock. The English had been singing hymns, including [some by] a fine quartet. On our side too the beautiful old songs resounded, with only now and then a shot in between."

Since the beginning of the war, the weather had been unusually warm and wet. But on December 24, the temperature dropped suddenly and a light snow fell. This certainly gave the area around

German soldiers getting ready for Christmas (THE GRANGER COLLECTION)

the trenches more of the look and feel of Christmas, but more important, the muddy ground began to freeze solid. For the first time in months, the men could move about in the trenches with relative ease.

As the sun began to set on Christmas Eve, the British High Command tried once again to keep the men on alert, hoping to discourage fraternization. A message was sent to all units along the Western Front: "It is thought possible that the enemy may be contemplating an attack during Xmas or New Year. Special vigilance will be maintained during this period."

The German High Command also wanted its soldiers on alert and ready to fight. Just before moving into the trenches that night, Private Hugo Klemm and his comrades were issued a warning: "[Our company commander] emphasized that for that day and the following days special alertness would be required, as it was expected that the English would perhaps take advantage of our good mood at Christmas by mounting a raid."

That night, all along the Western Front, the German soldiers entered the trenches carrying their weapons as well as some items their commanders would have frowned upon had they known.

A young German lieutenant recalled that "at darkness we marched forward . . . like Father Christmas with parcels hanging from us. All was quiet. No shooting. Little snow. We posted a tiny Christmas tree in our dugout [and] we placed a second lighted tree on the breastwork."

Winter's icy grip has taken hold of this Belgian trench at Nieuport.

(AUTHOR'S COLLECTION)

Across the way, British private Albert Moren glanced over the parapet of his trench toward the German lines. "It was a beautiful moonlit night," he wrote home, "frost on the ground, white almost everywhere; and about seven or eight in the evening there was a lot of commotion in the German trenches and there were these lights — I don't know what they were. And then [the Germans] sang 'Silent Night.' . . ."

Five miles south of Moren, another British soldier, Graham Williams, was on guard duty in a forward trench. "I was standing on the firestep, gazing towards the German lines and thinking what a different sort of Christmas Eve this was from any I had experienced in the past. . . . Then suddenly lights began to appear along the German parapet, which were evidently make-shift Christmas trees, adorned with lighted candles, which burnt steadily in the still, frosty air! Other sentries had, of course, seen the same thing, and quickly awoke those . . . asleep in the shelters, to 'come and see this thing, which had come to pass.'"

Williams and the men in his company watched as more trees appeared along the enemy's battle line. Then, suddenly, "our opponents began to sing 'Stille Nacht, Heilige Nacht.' . . . They finished their carol and we thought that we ought to retaliate in the same way, so we sang 'The First Nowell,' and when we finished that they all began clapping. And so it went on. First the Germans would sing one of their carols and then we would sing one of ours, until when we started up 'O Come All Ye Faithful' the Germans immediately joined in singing the same hymn to the Latin words *'Adeste Fideles.'* And I thought, well, this was really a most extraordinary thing — two nations both singing the same carol in the middle of a war."

As midnight approached, both sides held religious ceremonies to celebrate the holiday and to remember their fallen comrades. Barns

Two British soldiers bringing in mistletoe (MARY EVANS PICTURE LIBRARY)

German soldiers singing Christmas carols on Christmas Eve, 1914 (THE GRANGER COLLECTION)

behind the trenches were cleared of debris to become makeshift chapels, with wooden tables as an altar and candles stuck in dusty wine bottles.

A Belgian captain, Robert de Wilde, was relieved that the Germans did not launch an artillery attack during their evening services. Instead, the Germans sent up numerous rocket flares to light up the horizon a joyous blue. When de Wilde heard the enemy singing carols, he was overcome with emotion. "It was unreal, sublime. . . . The Christmases of long ago were coming to life again, all the things we had known in our childhood, the family, the countryside, the fireside, our eyes dazzled by the tree with its sparkling candles. . . ."

A French officer told about an outdoor service held just 150 feet from the German trenches. "Throughout the whole ceremony, the Boches . . . did not fire a single shot. For an instant the God of goodwill was once more master of this corner of the earth."

In a few places, something remarkable took place. Soldiers from both sides got out of their trenches and cautiously walked into No Man's Land. Meeting in the middle, they would shake hands, exchange cigars or tins of food, and chat. Despite obvious language barriers, a number of these meetings produced promises to continue the peace on Christmas Day.

But peace was not on everyone's mind that night. There were still many places along the line where machine-gun and rifle fire broke the silence. One English officer wanted to shoot down the Christmas tree that sparkled on the enemy parapet across from him. "I was for not allowing the blighters to enjoy themselves," this anonymous officer complained, "especially as they had killed one of our men that afternoon. But my captain . . . wouldn't let me shoot."

The peace was indeed a very fragile one. As a French officer observed, "It would be so easy to put an end to this scene; one salvo from our sector . . ."

Even as the officer wrote this, a shot rang out. "Bang!" his account continues. "A shot has been fired. Oh, the folly of that bullet

A star shell lights up the sky over the trenches at Ploegsteert, Belgium.

(IMPERIAL WAR MUSEUM, Q445)

which has torn the air apart and perhaps reached its target. All at once their singing stops. . . . What a pity."

Among German troops, a similar nervous hope existed. One officer wondered, "Is it possible? Are the French really going to leave us in peace today, Christmas Eve? Is it our imagination or is it maybe meant to lull us into a false sense of security? We all kept on our guard. . . ."

An uneasy sort of peace had been achieved for the night. But as the soldiers went to sleep, they wondered what Christmas Day would bring. Just in case, they kept their machine guns and rifles at their sides, loaded and ready for action.

FIVE

IT WAS A SIGHT ONE WILL NEVER SEE AGAIN

On Christmas morning, the men awoke to something strange. Absolute quiet. When they glanced over the parapets, they discovered a silent world covered by a thick, clinging fog.

English lieutenant Edward Hulse noted that "the silence seemed extraordinary after the usual din. From all sides birds seemed to arrive, and we hardly ever see a bird generally. Later in the day I fed about fifty sparrows outside my dugout, which shows you how complete the silence and quiet was."

An English sergeant, Alfred Self, was a bit unnerved by the lack of familiar battle noise. "It was so quiet, it was uncanny," he wrote in his diary. "There were no planes overhead, no observation balloons, no bombs, no rifle fire, therefore no snipers, just an occasional lark. . . ."

Some men looked out on this strange scene and wondered if they had entered a dream world. Others prayed that the peaceful atmosphere would continue. As the fog began to lift, soldiers became aware of movement along the enemy trenches.

In one area of the battle line, German soldiers noticed that a wooden board was being held up by British soldiers with the words

An artist's conception of the beginning of the Christmas Truce

(*ILLUSTRATED LONDON NEWS*/MARY EVANS PICTURE LIBRARY)

MERRY CHRISTMAS written on it. Several miles away, another board appeared on the German side that read, YOU NO FIGHT, WE NO FIGHT.

A junior officer remembered that when the fog cleared he saw a number of German soldiers doing exercises. "They waved," he wrote, "and our men waved back; after all it was Christmas Day. . . ." A few minutes passed without anyone firing a shot and then suddenly "the Germans opposite to us and our men were meeting in No Man's Land."

In other places where the men were more cautious, it took a while before trust won out. A British soldier, Wilbert Spencer, noted that "there was no firing, so by degrees each side began gradually showing more of themselves, and two of their men came halfway and called for an officer."

German and British officers mingle in No Man's Land.

(IMPERIAL WAR MUSEUM, Q50721)

School Library Media Center
34 Farms Village Road
Simsbury, CT 06070

Spencer could speak German fluently, so he "went out and found that they were willing to have an armistice for [four] hours. . . . This I arranged and then — can you imagine? — both sides came out, met in the middle, shook hands, wished each other compliments of the season, and had a chat. A strange sight between two hostile lines."

Two British riflemen (on the left) with a group of German soldiers

(IMPERIAL WAR MUSEUM, Q11718)

There had been no official declaration of a universal truce. In fact, commanders had gone out of their way to forbid any stopping of the fighting. And yet more such truces — hundreds of them — were arranged that Christmas morning all along the Western Front. Some truces were arranged by posting a sign suggesting a cease-fire. Others came about through shouted negotiations between lines or simply because soldiers wandered into No Man's Land and weren't shot.

These truces were arranged so quickly that high-ranking officers could do little to prevent them. Lieutenant Colonel Charles McLean was making his daily tour of the trenches when he spotted some of his men clambering over the top and wandering toward the enemy. He ran along the trenches, shouting for his men to return, but they ignored his instructions. When he kept on insisting that they come back, his men pointed out that "a number of the enemy were out on their side and gazing peacefully across."

The idea of a truce during a war wasn't new or unusual. Truces had been called in fighting as far back as the Battle of Thermopylae in 480 BC. During the American Civil War, numerous truces were arranged to bury the dead and to remove the wounded from the battlefields. Most such truces were approved by the officers for a limited amount of time and for very specific reasons. The Christmas Truce of 1914, however, was unique. While some senior officers went out of their way to "look the other way," most officers worked hard to put an end to it. The fact that the men under them

British and German soldiers exchange gifts in No Man's Land.

In the background, one soldier reads an enemy newspaper.

(*ILLUSTRATED LONDON NEWS*/MARY EVANS PICTURE LIBRARY)

defied these orders is extremely unusual. In addition, this truce lasted much longer and involved many more soldiers than any other previous truce.

At the French village of New Houplines on the River Lys, Captain C. I. Stockwell was shocked when five Germans began rolling a large barrel of beer across No Man's Land. "A lot more Saxons then appeared without arms. Things were getting a bit thick. My men were getting a bit excited, and the Saxons kept shouting to them to come out. We did not like to fire as they were all unarmed, but we had strict orders and someone might have fired, so I climbed over the parapet and shouted . . . for the opposing Captain to appear."

Neither captain spoke the other's language, but the meeting that followed produced an informal peace. Each side agreed to refrain from shooting until the following day. Then the German captain gave the beer to Captain Stockwell and received a generous supply of plum pudding in exchange.

While some regiments along the Western Front refused to take part, a startling number of men on both sides seemed to embrace the peace wholeheartedly. Ten minutes after agreeing to a cease-fire, Dougan Chater reported that "the ground between the two lines of trenches was swarming with men and officers of both sides, shaking hands and wishing each other a happy Christmas."

After the initial friendly meetings, the men realized there was a grim task to perform. Daylight and the walk into No Man's Land had allowed them to see the bodies of dead comrades still on the battlefield.

In some sections of the front lines, only a few bodies were to be found. But in areas where the recent large-scale charges had taken place, there were often scores of dead to bury. "It was

Soldiers preparing for the joint burial of comrades who died during a nighttime charge on December 18 (IMPERIAL WAR MUSEUM, Q50720)

heartrending," English captain Giles Loder wrote in his war diary, "to see some of the chaps one knew so well, and who had started out in such good spirits . . . lying there dead."

Soldiers then began the sad job of locating dead comrades and carrying them back to their side of the battle line. While this was being done, other soldiers dug graves out of the now-frozen earth and the dead were buried.

No army photographers were present during the Christmas Truce, so most of the photos of the event were taken by amateurs and are dark and a little out of focus.

(IMPERIAL WAR MUSEUM, Q50719)

Following the burials, the men on both sides usually held separate prayer services for their fallen comrades. A nineteen-year-old British lieutenant, Arthur Pelham-Burn, described a "most wonderful joint burial service" he participated in for one hundred dead British and German soldiers. "Our Padre . . . arranged the prayers and psalm etc. and an interpreter wrote them out in German. They

were read first in English by our Padre and then in German by a [German] boy who was studying for the ministry. It was an extraordinary and most wonderful sight. The Germans formed up on one side, the English on the other, the officers standing in front, every head bared. Yes, I think it was a sight one will never see again."

Once the burials and services were finished, the soldiers mingled in the blasted area between the lines. Small gifts were presented to the enemy, such as jam, cigars, cigarettes, chocolate, coffee, sausages, nuts, tea, and newspapers. Many soldiers exchanged souvenirs, including regimental badges and buttons cut off their uniforms. One of the most highly prized items was a *Pickelhaube*, the spiked helmet that was still in use by the German army early in the war.

In one spot, a pair of rabbits suddenly began running across No Man's Land and the men took off after them. A British private found it "laughable to see the Germans and ourselves helter-skelter after the Christmas dinner, which escaped." The regimental history of one English company recorded that a pig was killed, then "cooked . . . in No Man's Land and shared . . . with the Boche."

Many strange and unusual things were observed that day. Bruce Bairnsfather was amazed when he saw "one of my machine-gunners . . . cutting the unnaturally long hair of a docile Boche, who was patiently kneeling on the ground whilst the automatic clippers crept up the back of his neck."

While scenes like this were being played out in many locations, there were other areas where the fighting went on as always. In most cases it was the Germans who made the suggestion for a day of peace, only to be rejected. An English major was in no mood for an armistice when "at daybreak a few Germans put their heads up and shouted 'Merry Xmas.' Our men, after yesterday, were not feeling that way, and shot at them. They at once replied and a sniping match went on all day."

Two German officers (in forefront) and two British soldiers pose for a picture. (IMPERIAL WAR MUSUEM, Q11719)

A photograph of British and German troops (JOHN FROST HISTORICAL NEWSPAPER LIBRARY)

Several miles away, Captain Billy Congreve noted in his diary: "We have issued orders to the men not on any account to allow a 'truce,' as we have heard that they will probably try to. The Germans did try. They came over towards us singing. So we opened rapid fire on them, which is the only truce they deserve."

While it was usually the Allies who refused to have a truce, there were a few places where the Germans were the ones who wanted to continue the fighting. A German lieutenant sent a formal refusal to a British truce offer that said in part: "Gentlemen — You asked us yesterday temporarily to suspend hostilities and to become friends during Christmas. Such a proposal in the past would have been accepted with pleasure, but at the present time, when we have clearly recognized England's real character, we refuse to make any such arrangement."

And, of course, individuals in German units often boycotted the truce. One of the most infamous was a young corporal of an infantry regiment that was a mile or so from the front lines. When his comrades heard about the truce, they suggested marching forward to join the celebration. Corporal Adolf Hitler firmly refused to take part, arguing that "Such a thing should never happen in wartime. Have you no German sense of honor left at all?"

In the end, however, it was peace that won the day as hundreds of thousands of soldiers simply decided, despite direct orders to the contrary, that they weren't going to fight. As a surprised Corporal Stephen Coy reported, "The Germans are 'fed up' with the war, and will not fire unless British soldiers do. They admit they have been bluffed by the Kaiser. . . . One fellow, who was a teacher in England, when asked what he thought of the war, said — 'The war is finished here. We don't want to shoot.'"

A British private was startled when he greeted a German in No Man's Land. "The first man I came to was an old man, and when we shook hands I thought he was not going to let my hand go. The tears came rolling down his cheeks, and I felt sorry for him as he was so old, and wanted to go home."

As night approached, many of the men began drifting back to their trenches. "Altogether we had a great day with our enemies," British private P. H. Jones wrote in his diary, "and parted with much handshaking and mutual goodwill."

In Dougan Chater's section, the men arranged to have another truce on New Year's Day. Evidently, a number of photographs had been taken that day and "the Germans wanted to [return to] see how they [came] out."

There was a realization on both sides that something truly extraordinary had taken place. A German soldier wrote home that "it was a Christmas celebration in keeping with the command 'Peace on earth' and a memory which will stay with us always." His view was echoed by a British soldier: "This experience has been the most practical demonstration I have seen of 'Peace on earth and goodwill towards men.' " British sergeant Alfred Lovell returned to his dugout to record his thoughts: "Even as I write I can scarcely credit what I have seen and done. This has indeed been a wonderful day."

As darkness once again embraced the quiet battlefield, the armies settled in for a night's rest. British captain R. J. Armes found it difficult to sleep, so he wandered along the trench, thinking about what he had just experienced. "I left our friends [the Germans] on Xmas Day in a quiet mood. I stood upon the parapet & had a final look around and not a shot was fired."

THE LULL IS FINISHED

Back at headquarters, General Horace Smith-Dorrien had been receiving disturbing reports all day about strange goings-on at the front. Fighting had all but ground to a halt, and the opposing armies were having friendly meetings in No Man's Land. Smith-Dorrien fired off an angry message to his commanders: "I have issued the strictest orders that on no account is [fraternization] to be allowed between the opposing troops. To finish this war quickly, we must keep up the fighting spirit and do all we can to discourage friendly [meetings]."

Because Smith-Dorrien had also heard that some officers were actually encouraging the truce, he issued an ominous warning: "I am calling for particulars as to names of officers and units who took part in this Christmas gathering, with a view to disciplinary action."

The commander of all British troops, Field Marshall John French, was just as angry. "When this [fraternization] was reported to me I issued immediate orders to prevent any recurrence of such conduct, and called the local commanders to strict account, which resulted in a good deal of trouble."

General Horace Smith-Dorrien was adamant that his troops would not
fraternize with the enemy. (NATIONAL PORTRAIT GALLERY, LONDON)

The German High Command took much the same view and issued a terse order: "Commander Second Army directs that informal understandings with enemy are to cease. Officers . . . allowing them are to be brought before a court-martial."

In some areas, these orders had immediate results. British private Bernard Brookes was standing guard at midnight on December 25 when "our artillery sent over . . . four shells of small caliber to let

them know that the truce, at which the whole world would wonder, was ended, and in its place, Death and Bloodshed would once again reign supreme." The Germans countered with an artillery barrage of their own.

Despite the urgings of officers to fire on the enemy, many soldiers on both sides were reluctant to give up the peace. Some simply didn't fire at the enemy. British private William Tapp related that

Second Lieutenant Cyril Drummond thought the Germans "were very nice fellows. . . . [So] I lined them all up and took a photograph."
(IMPERIAL WAR MUSUEM, HU35801)

opposing troops were still meeting in No Man's Land as the sun came up on December 26. "It's too ridiculous for words," he noted, "we are all mixing up again."

At nine o'clock that morning, the Allied commanding officers ordered an artillery duel. Tapp continued his report: "Shells are exchanged for a few hours but [every so often] we all stand up. . . . No fear of being shot with a bullet."

At another spot in the line, two opposing officers met, and the German informed his British counterpart that "his Colonel had given orders for a renewal of hostilities at mid-day and might the men be warned to keep down, please?" The British officer thanked him for the warning and returned to his trench. Then, just before the shooting was to start, a tin was thrown into the British trench with a message that read: *We shoot to the air.* "And sure enough," the English regiment's history records, "at the appointed hour a few vague shots were fired high over the trenches. Then all was quiet again and the unofficial truce continued."

On the German side, resistance to resuming the fighting was even stronger. One British unit's war diary states simply that "The Germans throughout the morning appeared to have *no intention* of opening fire on us."

In another section, the order to fire on the British nearly caused a mutiny. "When the order to fire was given," a German officer told Ethel Cooper years later, "the men struck. . . . The officers . . . stormed up and down, and got, as the only result, the answer, 'We can't — they are good fellows, and we can't.' Finally, the officers threatened the men with, 'Fire, or we do — and not at the *enemy*!' Not a shot had come from the other side, but at last [we] fired, and an answering fire came back, but not a man fell. We spent that day and the next wasting ammunition in trying to shoot the stars down from the sky."

There was some attempt to restart the war following Christmas. Several small raids were launched, and the artillery on both sides sent shells screaming through the air. Even so, many of the men still managed to arrange a number of informal truces on New Year's Eve and New Year's Day. These truces did not involve nearly as many men as those at Christmas. In addition to the raids and shelling, a good number of the units on both sides that had taken part in the first truce were reassigned to other sections of the battlefield. This separated opponents who had gotten to know and like one another.

Despite an increasing movement back to fighting, some areas held on to their truces for as long as possible. In Ploegsteert Wood in Belgium, for instance, little hard fighting took place until early spring. "The truce continues," an amazed corporal noted in his diary. "Starting with the 'peace and goodwill' idea on Christmas Day, it was found mutually pleasant and convenient that neither side, though keeping close watch, fires a shot."

Following Christmas, the warm weather and rain returned. The terrible mud that had made their lives miserable before Christmas

A group of relaxed and contented soldiers in Ploegsteert Wood in Belgium
(IMPERIAL WAR MUSEUM, Q11729)

also reappeared. British captain Maurice Mascall thought the extended peace a practical and sensible idea. "There is no sniping, and the men of both sides stand up and repair their parapets, and wave to each other, and sometimes make each other tea, and it is all most gentlemanly! Also it is very sensible, as this useless and annoying sniping can have no real effect on the progress of the campaign."

A genuine friendship developed between the English and German soldiers in Ploegsteert Wood. Because an inspection by a high-ranking officer meant the men would have to demonstrate a fighting spirit by firing at the enemy, both sides took to informing the other of such visits. Lieutenant J. D. Wyatt recalled the day when "a message came down the line to say that the Germans [expected] that their General was coming along in the afternoon, so we had better keep down, as they might have to do a little shooting to make things look right!!! And this is war!!"

The peace in Ploegsteert lasted throughout March and caused Captain Mascall to exclaim, "Isn't this an extraordinary state of affairs! [The Germans] seem to get more friendly every day, and Heaven knows how they will ever start fighting again."

Such comments were precisely what the military commanders feared and prompted General Horace Smith-Dorrien to rage, "War to the knife is the only way to carry on a campaign of this sort!"

By Easter, the truces were all over. Artillery barrages became common again, and the snipers went out to do their methodical, deadly work. An editorial in the *London Daily Mirror* lamented the turn of events: "But now an end to the truce. The news, bad and good, begins again. 1915 darkens over. Again we who watch have to mourn many of our finest men. The lull is finished. The absurdity and the tragedy renew themselves."

There would be a few small, isolated truces during Christmas 1915 but nothing at all like what had happened the year before.

Anticipating another attempt at fraternization, the commanders of all armies issued strict warnings against such shows of friendship. To further discourage meetings in No Man's Land, the 1915 Christmas season was marked by continual artillery barrages.

The Great War would drag along for another four years. Many

Soon after the Christmas Truce, officers on both sides restarted the war. Here, British and Canadian troops are in a pitched battle near Ypres. (AUTHOR'S COLLECTION)

more desperate, futile charges would be mounted, answered by just as many countercharges. All were aimed at breaking through the enemy's line and destroying their will to fight. Very little territory was actually gained by either side during this time, and it seemed as if the fighting would drag along for many more years.

Everything changed when the United States entered the war against Germany, Austria, and their allies in 1917. The United States lent money to the Allied countries and began sending them badly needed war supplies. Much more important, three million American troops would join the Allied soldiers in battle.

Exhausted by war and a decimated army, Emperor Charles I of Austria (who had become emperor in 1916 when his eighty-five-year-old great-uncle Franz Josef died) sought peace in October 1918. Kaiser Wilhelm found himself faced with mutinies in both his army and navy, political unrest at home, and an advancing enemy. He abdicated his throne in November and then Germany sued for peace. When the war finally ended in 1918, the front lines were remarkably similar to those that existed in 1914.

The carnage and destruction were appalling. Over eight million soldiers had been killed by bombardment, machine-gun and rifle fire, poison gas, and disease. Another six-and-a-half million civilians also perished. Cities and villages were leveled, farms and factories blown to pieces. Where crops had once grown, endless lines of simple white crosses now dotted the landscape.

Hundreds of thousands of soldiers who survived the war returned home with ghastly physical wounds. Many others suffered lifelong emotional damage from what they had witnessed and endured. The number of casualties was so high that by 1918, both sides — soldiers and civilians alike — were angry and vengeful. But not at their own political leaders for getting them into war under false pretenses or at their military commanders for sticking with clearly outmoded and deadly combat tactics. At the time, most people still believed their country's propaganda; instead, they blamed their enemies for the slaughter and demanded justice.

The ruined village of Athies, France, with a huge crater in the center, was an all too typical scene after the war. (IMPERIAL WAR MUSEUM, Q1941)

Europe After the War

After the war, many of the names and borders of countries changed.

Charles I was banished from Austria and spent the rest of his brief life living in poverty on the island of Madeira; after abdicating, Kaiser Wilhelm went into exile in Holland. Two other empires also fell apart as a result of the war. The Ottoman Empire was dissolved when it surrendered to the Allies in 1918 and eventually became the Republic of Turkey. In Russia, Bolshevik revolutionaries and a mutinous army forced Czar Nicholas II to give up the throne in 1917, and the Union of Soviet Socialist Republics was created. The czar and his entire family were assassinated a year later, ending three hundred years of imperial rule.

In an effort to weaken Germany and ensure a peaceful future, the Allies insisted that Germany and Austria give up territory to create a number of new and independent countries. Millions of Germans and Austrians suddenly found themselves being ruled by people they had formerly considered inferior to them.

Germany came in for additional sanctions, which included surrendering all its overseas colonies and sharply reducing its military forces and equipment. It was also required to pay reparations (for the expense of damages caused by the war, plus pensions for the soldiers and widows of its enemies), "a sum," historian Michael Howard noted, "so huge that it could not even be computed." Finally, and possibly most galling to the Germans, they were required to admit that the war had been their fault alone.

German representatives at the negotiations protested the harsh terms, especially what came to be known as the "war guilt" clause. But with their army in disarray and tens of thousands of citizens near starvation, they had no other choice but to agree to sign the Versailles Treaty. Far from breaking the German spirit, the treaty embittered that country's people and made them determined to

regain their former power. These feelings eventually led the German people to back a political extremist named Adolf Hitler and resulted, twenty years later, in World War II.

How would history have been changed if Kaiser Wilhelm had been less arrogant and aggressive or had not egged on Emperor Franz Josef? Could the First World War have been avoided if the kaiser had only read the Serbian response to Austria-Hungary's ultimatum sooner? What might have happened if the war had been delayed long enough for the less warlike Charles I to take the Austrian throne?

Many historians would brush aside such questions as foolish "what if" history and argue that Germany and Austria were determined to go to war to achieve their national goals. And the truth is that we have no idea whether or not the First World War could have been avoided if each country's leader had been more willing to reason rather than fight. But at least one future British prime minister, Winston Churchill, did ask a hypothetical question that bears thinking about. "What would happen," he wondered one month before the Christmas Truce of 1914, "if the armies suddenly and simultaneously went on strike . . . ?"

British private Albert Moren had an answer to the question: "If the truce had gone on and on, there's no telling what could have

Many viewed World War I as senseless, and a strong antiwar campaign developed during the war. This cartoon, entitled "The Harvest Is Ripe," shows the Grim Reaper mowing down rows of human beings. (THE GRANGER COLLECTION)

happened," Moren replied. "It could have meant the end of the war. After all they didn't want war, and we didn't want war and it could have ended up by finishing the war altogether."

Major Murdoch McKenzie Wood had an even stronger opinion. Wood was in the trenches in 1914 and had participated in a truce that lasted over two weeks. "I . . . came to the conclusion that I have held firmly ever since, that if we had been left to ourselves there would have never been another shot fired. For a fortnight that truce went on. We were on the most friendly terms, and it was only the fact that we were being controlled by others that made it necessary for us to start trying to shoot one another again."

After word of the truce reached England, the *Herald* newspaper's editorial writer rejoiced that peace could win out, even if only for a few days. "It is especially saddening," the editorial lamented, "that such soldiers are not in charge of the affairs of Europe instead of the diplomats and potentates. If they were we would have a natural and human Europe."

A soldier stops at the grave of a fallen comrade.

(IMPERIAL WAR MUSEUM, Q13378)

EPILOGUE

Awhile back when I began doing research on the First World War, I focused on the vital and heroic role played by the more than 400,000 African-American soldiers in that war. I was deep into this line of study when I realized something. Since I'd begun my readings, a number of very good books on the subject had appeared for young readers, most notably Walter Dean Myers' *The Harlem Hellfighters: When Pride Met Courage* and Michael Cooper's *Hell Fighters: African American Soldiers in World War I*.

Instead of abandoning the First World War completely, I continued to read books and articles about the conflict. At the time, this was a journey of exploration only. I gathered information about the soldiers and what life at the front was like; I learned about the weapons used and the horrible wounds they inflicted. Then amid all this destruction and death I came across an amazing moment in the war — a time when tens of thousands of troops on both sides simply refused to fight.

I first found references to what came to be called the "Christmas Truce" in Martin Gilbert's remarkable book *The First World War: A Complete History*. Here was an astonishing event that highlighted all of the best qualities of the human spirit and, incidentally, provided me with a new focus for my research.

But maybe even as striking was Gilbert's description of the events that led up to the conflict — the unbearably tense atmosphere in Europe that existed in the early years of the twentieth century and what seemed like a blind race to war following the assassination of Franz Ferdinand. It struck me that in a real way these emotions and events paralleled events in our own time.

Following the tragic attacks of September 11, 2001, the media was flooded with information from our government about "weapons of mass destruction," how certain countries hated the United States and were happy to see us attacked, and how terrorists were already among us and might strike at any moment. Frequently, messages demonized certain Islamic countries, suggesting unfairly that all Muslims were in some way linked to the attacks. The implication was fairly obvious: We needed to do something to them before they did anything else to us.

Elements of the discussion were true. There really were some people who wanted us attacked. But other aspects of this prewar rhetoric — in particular, the idea that the enemy was building weapons of mass destruction — proved to be false.

Some people here at home and even some other governments tried to slow the march to war by urging a careful look at the actual evidence. This advice was pushed aside, the sad result of lingering anger over the September 11 attacks, fear of the unknown, and a widespread suspicion of Muslims. The war in Iraq was launched with a real sense that it would be short and decisive and that we would soon be safe from our enemies.

But as in World War I, this national optimism soon collided head-on with reality. Shortly after hostilities began, our president declared an end to major combat operations while standing underneath a MISSION ACCOMPLISHED banner. It was only then that the real war began — a brutal hit-and-run contest that has lasted many years, claimed the lives of thousands of American soldiers, more than one hundred and fifty thousand Iraqi civilians, and devastated a country's economy and landscape.

It is always risky to compare one war to another. The issues, cultures, and personalities are usually quite different and some wars are justified (such as the Second World War against Hitler and his allies) while others are not. But there is no reason why lessons can't be drawn from history. World War I might very well have happened anyway, but it is fair to ask how the world would have been different if the sides involved had been more willing to sit down and negotiate their differences. At the very least, the Christmas Truce of World War I demonstrated that the combatants were more alike than not. It may have been a small step toward peace on earth, a tiny bit of light in a vast and threatening darkness, but it offered reassurance and hope that a kinder, humane spirit could prevail amid the horrible brutality of war.

TIME LINE

June 28 — Archduke Franz Ferdinand and his wife are assassinated in Sarajevo, the capital of Bosnia-Herzegovina.

July 23 — Austria-Hungary delivers ultimatum to Serbia and demands an answer within 48 hours.

July 25 — The Serbians agree to meet all but one of the demands in the Austria-Hungary ultimatum. The emperor of Austria-Hungary, Franz Joseph, rejects the Serbian response and mobilizes his army. Russia's Czar Nicholas II mobilizes part of his forces to protect its border from a joint German/Austro-Hungarian attack. Germany and Italy threaten to mobilize their armies if Russia continues to prepare for war.

July 28 — Austria-Hungary declares war on Serbia.

July 29 — Austrian-Hungarian warships on the Danube River bombard the Serbian capital of Belgrade. Serbian artillery responds.

July 30 — Russia mobilizes all troops.

August 1 — France mobilizes its army after Germany demands that it surrender its border forts. Germany mobilizes its army.

August 2 — German troops occupy neutral Luxembourg and demand free passage through Belgium. Turkey aligns itself with Germany to head off a possible Russian attack.

August 3 — Germany declares war against France. Belgian government rejects the German demand to allow its forces free passage through Belgian territory. German troops invade Belgium. Britain mobilizes its forces. Turkey mobilizes its forces.

August 4 — Britain declares war on Germany.

August 5 — Montenegro declares war on Austria-Hungary.

August 6 — Austria-Hungary declares war on Russia.

August 6 — Serbia declares war on Germany. German army breaks through Belgian border defenses though their advance is slowed by heavy resistance.

August 7 — 120,000 British soldiers reach France.

August 8 — French army advances against German forces in Alsace, beginning a series of battles along the French and Belgian borders.

August 10 — France declares war on Austria-Hungary. Turkey declares war on Britain and its allies.

August 12 — Britain declares war on Austria-Hungary.

August 12–21 — 200,000 troops from Austria-Hungary invade Serbia.

August 14–22 — Two French armies advance into Lorraine. The German army there begins a careful withdrawal to allow reinforcements to arrive. A German counterattack on August 20 drives the French army back, but defeat is avoided when the French hold the high ground outside the city of Nancy.

August 15 — Japan demands that Germany evacuate its colonies in China.

August 16 — All of Belgium's border defenses fall and its army begins withdrawing as the German army pushes westward.

August 17–19 — Russian forces invade northeast Germany but are stopped by a strong German counterattack.

August 18 — The Belgian army is trapped near the port of Antwerp. A portion of the German army is left to contain them there, while the rest of the German army continues moving toward the French/Belgian border.

August 19 — German troops shoot 150 Belgian civilians in order to stop nonmilitary resistance to the invasion.

August 20 — German forces occupy Brussels, the capital of Belgium.

August 20–25 — German army moves into the Ardennes region, inflicting severe losses on the outnumbered French forces there. The French begin to withdraw.

August 22–23 — Three German armies enter France. French resistance is fierce but can't stop the forward movement of the Germans. French forces begin to retreat.

August 23 — The British forces engage the German army at Mons, Belgium. After a fierce fight they are forced to make an orderly retreat.

August 25–27 — British troops continue to retreat and are routed at Le Cateau, France.

August 26–30 — Russian troops suffer a severe beating in Prussia at the hands of German troops. To the southeast, Russian and Austrian-Hungarian armies have numerous battles; while none are decisive, the Russian forces seem to be prevailing.

August 29–September 2 — To aid the British withdrawal, the French launch an attack on the advancing Germans. Despite a fierce fight, parts of the German army are within fifty miles of Paris by September 2.

September 3–11 — Russian forces split the Austrian-Hungarian armies in two, forcing them to retreat. In battles in the area between Poland and Romania, Austria-Hungary has already lost over 350,000 men who were either killed, wounded, or taken prisoner.

September 4–14 — French and British launch a counterattack against the overextended German forces along the Marne River. By September 14, German forces are in retreat and the Schlieffen Plan is declared a failure.

September 7–17 — Austrian-Hungarian troops invade Serbia for a second time and after 10 days of fighting, force Serbian troops to withdraw to positions around Belgrade. Meanwhile, Belgian troops attack German forces near Antwerp, forcing Germany to bring in extra troops.

September 15–18 — A French and British attack on retreating German forces fails and is called off.

September 17 — Australia declares support for Britain. Germany rushes troops to southern Germany to support the badly beaten Austrian-Hungarian troops there.

September 22–November 12 — Numerous battles in France and Belgium result in high casualties but little change in the position of the armies. Both sides begin digging trenches that will soon stretch from the North Sea to the Swiss border.

November 13–December 24 — Few major battles are fought as lack of ammunition and fresh troops plus wet winter weather make such operations difficult. The First World War is five months old and already casualty figures are staggering. Serbia reports 170,000 killed, wounded, or taken prisoner; Austria-Hungary has suffered at least 1,250,000 casualties. Russia estimates losses at 1,800,000. On the Western Front, France, Britain, and Belgium have suffered more than 1,000,000 casualties, while Germany reports 950,000 killed or wounded.

December 25 — Weary from months of constant fighting, tens of thousands of soldiers on both sides call a series of impromptu truces.

The Christmas Truces provided a rare period of peace along many sections of the Western Front. But soon the fighting resumed with ferocious battles being fought just about every day for the next three years and eleven months. Of the 65 million soldiers who fought in the war, an estimated eight million were killed and 21 million wounded. An untold number of soldiers also suffered deep and lasting psychological scars. Civilian casualties were just as staggering with at least 6.5 million dying from wounds, disease, or starvation. The guns were finally stilled on November 11, 1918, when Germany admitted it could not win the war and signed the armistice ending hostilities at 11 A.M. On June 28, 1919, after months of heated negotiations, Germany, Austria-Hungary, Bulgaria, and Turkey signed the Treaty of Versailles; representatives from the 27 victorious countries countersigned the 200-page document, officially ending the First World War.

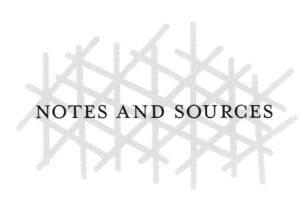

NOTES AND SOURCES

OPENING QUOTE

- Winston Churchill's letter to his wife can be found in Gilbert, Martin, *The First World War: A Complete History* (Henry Holt and Company, New York, NY, 1994), p. 25.

PREFACE

- The reference to Walter Limmer comes from Witkop, Philip (ed.), *German Students' War Letters* (Methuen Publishing, Ltd., London, 1929), p. 9.

- Dougan Chater's comment can be found in Brown, Malcolm and Seaton, Shirley, *Christmas Truce* (Pan Books, London, 2001), p. 8.

ONE: THOSE STUPID KINGS AND EMPERORS

- A very nice summary of pre-war Europe and the many alliances that were formed is in Howard, Michael, *The First World War* (Oxford University Press, New York, NY, 2003), pp. 1–19. A somewhat more detailed account can be found in Gilbert, *The First World War*, pp. 1–18. Also see Joll, James, *The Origins of the First World War* (Longman Publishing Group, London, 1989); Steiner, Zara S., *Britain and the Origins of the First World War* (Macmillan, London, 1977); and Westwell, Ian, *World War I Day by Day* (MBI Publishing Company, St. Paul, MN, 1999), pp. 6–9.

- Brown and Seaton's *Christmas Truce* includes a powerful chapter on the use of propaganda to create a climate of hate and to motivate citizens and soldiers to back a war, pp. 1–11. Howard's *The First World War* looks at this topic also and even includes a discussion of how hatred for the enemy was so intense that England's royal family effectively re-branded itself to mask its German origins, going from the House of Hanover to the House of Windsor, pp. 44–47.

- The assassination of Archduke Franz Ferdinand and the events leading up to the start of the war, including the fact that Kaiser Wilhelm might have headed off the war if he'd only read Serbia's reply to the Austrian ultimatum, is handled very concisely in Gilbert, *The First World War*, pp. 14–31.

- Churchill's quote can be found in Churchill, Winston, *The World Crisis*, vol. 1 (Thorton Butterworth, London, 1923), p. 104.

TWO: THINGS WERE BEGINNING TO LOOK UNPLEASANT

- Germany's Schlieffen Plan and the opening battles of the war are discussed in Mosier, John, *The Myth of the Great War: How the Germans Won the Battles and How the Americans Saved the Allies* (HarperCollins, New York, NY, 2001), pp. 32–38, 49–50, 67–100; Brown, Malcolm, *The Imperial War Museum Book of the Western Front* (Motorbooks International Publishers, Osceola, WI, 1993), pp. 3–39; Gilbert, *The First World War*, pp. 29, 30, 35–77; Howard, *The First World War*, pp. 24, 28, 34–39; and Westwell, *World War I Day by Day*, pp. 10–35.

- Mosier, *The Myth of the Great War*, contains detailed discussions of the powerful weapons used in WWI and the casualties caused by them. There are over one hundred references scattered throughout his book, so it is easiest to check the index under *artillery*, *machine guns*, and *rifles*.

- Harold Macmillan's quote comes from Brown and Seaton, *Christmas Truce,* p. 9 (Macmillan, London, 1966). Albert George's observations of the artillery duels are from Brown, *The Imperial War Museum Book of the Western Front*, pp. 9–11 and 13–15. Edward Spears's description of the retreat appeared in Spears, Edward, *1914: A Narrative of the Great Retreat* (Eyre and Spottiswoode, London, 1930), p. 47.

THREE: ALL ATTACKS ARE TO BE PUSHED TO THE EXTREME

- Valentine Fleming's comments about the blasted landscape around him are from his letter to Winston Churchill from November 1914. Gilbert, *The First World War*, pp. 115–117, also contains descriptions of the front.

- For detailed information on the building of trenches, the day-to-day routine of life there, the dangers of diseases and snipers, and what it was like to charge across No Man's Land, see Ellis, John, *Eye-Deep in Hell: Trench Warfare in World War I* (Johns Hopkins University Press, Baltimore, MD, 1976). Also see Brown and Seaton, *Christmas Truce*, pp. 12–27; Mosier, *The Myth of the Great War*, pp. 154, 157, 175, 197, 202, and 238; and Weintraub, Stanley, *Silent Night: The Story of the World War I Christmas Truce* (Penguin Books/Simon & Schuster, New York, NY, 2002), pp. 1–4.

- Friedrich von Bernhardi's quote comes from von Bernhardi, Freidrich, *Germany and the Next War* (Longmans, Green & Co., London, 1914).

FOUR: THERE IS NO LONGER ANY SENSE IN THIS BUSINESS

- The gradual humanizing of the enemy and pre-Christmas contact between the lines is handled in depth in Brown and Seaton, *Christmas Truce*, pp. 23–46; and Weintraub, *Silent Night*, pp. 1–23. Also see Brown, *The Imperial War Museum Book of the Western Front*, pp. 47–49; Ellis, *Eye-Deep in Hell*, pp. 170–173; and Gilbert, *The First World War*, pp. 117–119.

FIVE: IT WAS A SIGHT ONE WILL NEVER SEE AGAIN

- Discussions of the Christmas Truce and what happened in the days after can be found in Brown and Seaton, *Christmas Truce*, pp. 80–195, and Weintraub, *Silent Night*, pp. 52–155.

- Quotes in this chapter come from a variety of sources: R. J. Armes from a letter in the Staffordshire Regiment files; Bruce Bairnsfather from Bairnsfather, Bruce, *Bullets and Billets* (G. P. Putnam's Sons, New York, NY, 1917); Stephen Coy from a letter that appeared in *The Scotsman*, January 7, 1915; Billy Congreve from *Armageddon Road: A V.C.'s Diary 1914–1916*, Terry Norman, ed. (William Kimber & Co., London, 1982); Sir Edward Hulse from *Letters* (privately printed); Giles Loder from the Public Record Office WO95/1657; Alfred Lovell from a letter in the *Evening News*, January 2, 1915; Alfred Self and Wilbert Spencer from their accounts in the Imperial War Museum; and C. I. Stockwell from Dunn, J. C., *The War the Infantry Knew: A Chronicle of Service in France and Belgium* (Jane's Information Group, Inc., London, 1987).

SIX: THE LULL IS FINISHED

- Discussions of the remaining years of the war can be found in Brown, *The Imperial War Museum Book of the Western Front*; Gilbert, *The First World War*; Howard, *The First World War*; Mosier, *The Myth of the Great War*; and Westwell, *World War I Day by Day*.

- Casualty figures come from Mosier, *The Myth of the Great War*. Because he has well over one hundred references on the subject, it's best to study the index where information is broken down by country. Mosier also details his casualty sources on pp. 348–349.

- Howard, *The First World War*, provides a concise explanation of the Treaty of Versailles and its effects on Germany and the future of Europe, pp. 129–143, as does Gilbert, *The First World War*, pp. 500–524.

- Quotes found in this chapter come from a variety of sources: Ethel Cooper comes from Cooper, Caroline Ethel, *Behind the Lines: One Woman's War, 1914–1918* (Jill Norman & Hobhouse, London, 1982); John French from French, John, *1914* (Constable and Company, Ltd., London, 1919), and J. D. Wyatt from his account in the Imperial War Museum.

MORE ABOUT WORLD WAR I

The following is a compilation of fiction, poetry, movies, and Web sites that will let readers learn more about World War I and let them experience more clearly what soldiers did and felt.

BOOKS

- *All Quiet on the Western Front* by Erich Maria Remarque (Little, Brown and Company, 1929) Idealistic nineteen-year-old Paul Baumer enlists in the German Army and experiences the devastating physical and psychological effects of combat.

- *Company K* by William March (Smith and Haas, 1933) One hundred and twenty-three different U.S. soldiers tell what it was like to enlist, train, and fight in the Great War.

- *Death of a Hero* by Richard Aldington (Garden City Publishing Company, 1929) A young English artist, George Winterbourne, is sent to the front lines and soon becomes disillusioned by the war and what it does to the men around him.

- *The General* by C. S. Forester (1936) Follows the fighting career of an honest but stubborn field general who repeatedly orders attacks that condemn thousands of the troops under his command to pointless mutilation and death.

- *Generals Die in Bed* by Charles Yale Harrison (William Morrow, 1930) An unnamed Canadian soldier is numbed by the horrors of war and by the way generals will do and say anything to whip troops into a fighting frenzy.

- *Great Poets of World War I* by Jon Stallworthy (Carrol & Graff Publishers, 2002) Brief biographies of some of the greatest poets of World War I along with samples of their work and numerous photographs.

- *Three Soldiers* by John Dos Passos (George H. Doran Company, 1921) A grimly realistic depiction of three idealistic soldiers as they contend with the regimentation, violence, and boredom of army life during World War I.

- *To the Last Man* by Jeff Shaara (Ballantine Books, 2004) A shifting point of view allows readers to experience the war through the eyes of high-ranking officers and common soldiers alike.
- *Under Fire: The Story of a Squad* by Henri Barbusse (E. P. Dutton & Company, 1917) Follows a squad of French volunteer soldiers on the front line in France shortly after the German invasion.
- *War Novel* by Michael Foreman (Pavilian Books, 1993) A group of four young men (based on the author's uncles) eagerly enlist for "the grand adventure," only to find themselves in horrific battle. Includes a description of the Christmas Truce.

MOVIES

- *All Quiet on the Western Front* (1930) A haunting and powerful antiwar movie that is faithful to the Remarque novel of the same name (see above).
- *Grand Illusion* (1937) French prisoners of war attempt to escape their German guards. Shows how the old, gentlemanly "rules" of warfare completely changed during the bloody, muddy fighting of World War I.
- *Paths of Glory* (1957) An ambitious French general sends his troops on an impossible mission. When they fail, he demands that three be tried for cowardice and executed.
- *Sergeant York* (1940) Based on the life of one of the war's greatest heroes, this movie follows the transformation of York from a dedicated fighter to a soldier with grave doubts about the war.

WEB SITES

Each Web site offers a wide variety of information about World War I from trench warfare, to the weapons used, to analysis of individual battles and much, much, more. Most also contain numerous photographs and illustrations.

- www.worldwar1.com
- www.besthistorysites.net (information about WWI can be found under Modern History)
- www.lib.byu.edu/index.php/Main_Page
- www.warpoetry.co.uk

INDEX

PAGE NUMBERS IN **BOLD** INDICATE ILLUSTRATIONS

ACKNOWLEDGMENTS

I want to thank the following individuals and institutions for their generous help in rounding up information and images for this book. Luci Gosling, Business Development Manager, and Tom Gillmor, Head of Content, Mary Evans Picture Library; Lila Dlaboha, Deputy Director, Ellen Sandberg, Research and Permissions, Maggie Downing, Researcher, and Silka Quintero, The Granger Collection; Sam Salvidge, Historic Newspapers, London; Andrew from John Frost Newspapers; Laura Warren and Glyn Biesty, the Imperial War Museum, London; and the photographic services department of the National Portrait Gallery, London. I would like to offer special thanks to Dr. Michael Neiberg, Professor of History, University of Southern Mississippi, for his careful fact checking and consultation on my text, and to Scholastic librarians Karen Van Rossem and Kerry Prendergast for their constant, generous assistance and support.